Photos for Collage

Photographs and Quotes
for Use in Personal Art

Jan Phillips

ISBN-13: 978-1499747058
ISBN-10:1499747055

www.janphillips.com

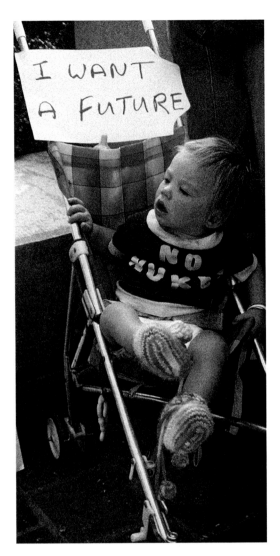

Dear Artist and Creator,

Over the years, I have had hundreds of collage artists in my workshops, and many of them were looking for copyright free images to use in their collages. I have put this book together to provide you with images and some quotations to use in your collages.

I would also suggest you visit the SoulCollage® Community at www.soulcollage.com. SoulCollage® is an intuitive process of self-discovery created by Seena Frost. My dear friend, Catherine Anderson, who inspired me to offer these images, is a trained facilitator and gifted teacher. She also has a book of images for collage available on Amazon called *Collage Imagery*.

Both of our books give permission to artists to cut the images out of our books and use them freely in your cards, collage art, journals or other art projects. You are also free to share your collage creations online without concern for copyright.

This is our way of supporting you in your creative work.

Have fun!

Jan Phillips
www.janphillips.com

Something deeply hidden had to be behind things.
Albert Einstein

God is experienced only in proportion as God is expressed.
Joel Goldsmith

Sometimes I go about
pitying myself,
and all along
my soul is being
blown by great winds
across the sky.

Ojibway saying

What we are looking for is Who is looking.

St. Francis of Assissi

THE WOMEN OF WORLD WAR II

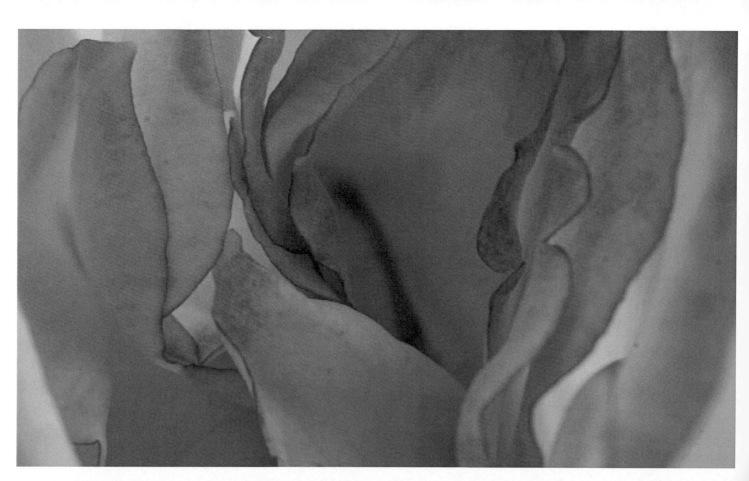

Probe every mystery.

I believe in myself, in my power, in my goodness.

Someone out there needs me.
I will live so they can find me.

What I create matters deeply.

Sanctify your own life,
value its worth.
Jan Phillips

Move only in the direction of your joy.

Creativity is work of the heart, unrelated to the
economy of our ordinary lives. It is not about ego,
not about money or success or failure.
It is a calling from the spirit, a chance at one
of life's powerful experiences,
to make something whole
from the pieces of our lives.

from *Marry Your Muse*

In the matter of the arts, before we can speak,
we must first hear. Before we can hear, we must
first be silent. And before we can be silent,
we must first leave the chaos.
Jan Phillips

Any space is sacred the moment
we declare it so.

No matter how brilliant our attempts to inform,
it is our ability to inspire that will turn the tides.
Jan Phillips

It may be that God is the impulse to laugh.
Rumi

If you don't know where you're going, you will probably end up somewhere else.
Laurence Johnston Peter

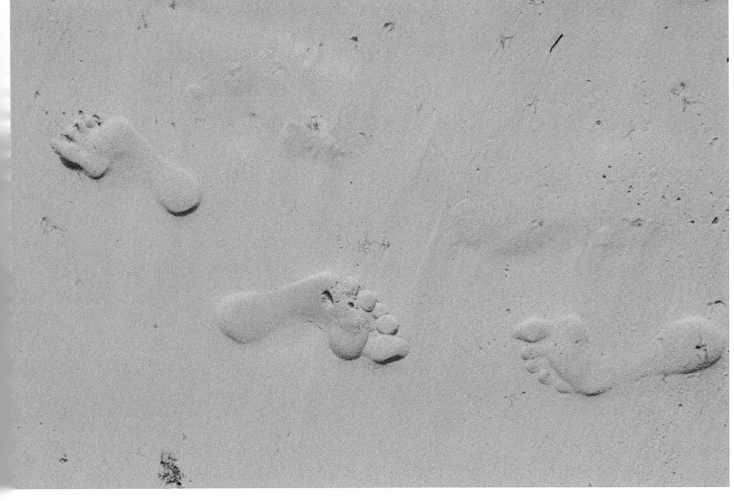

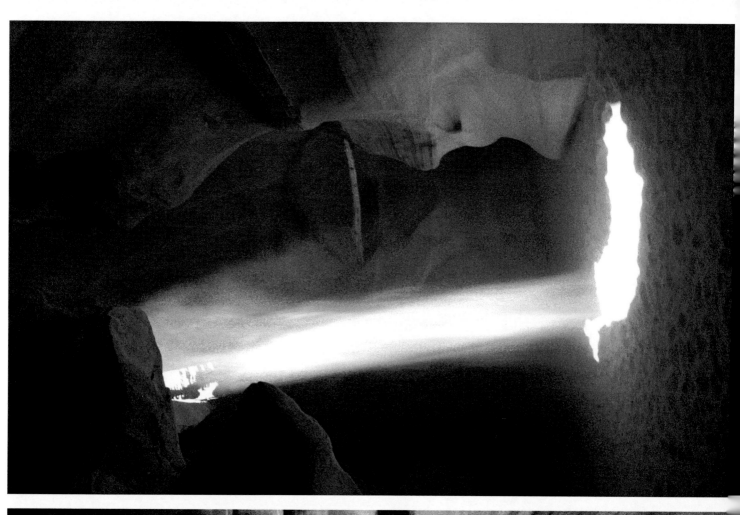

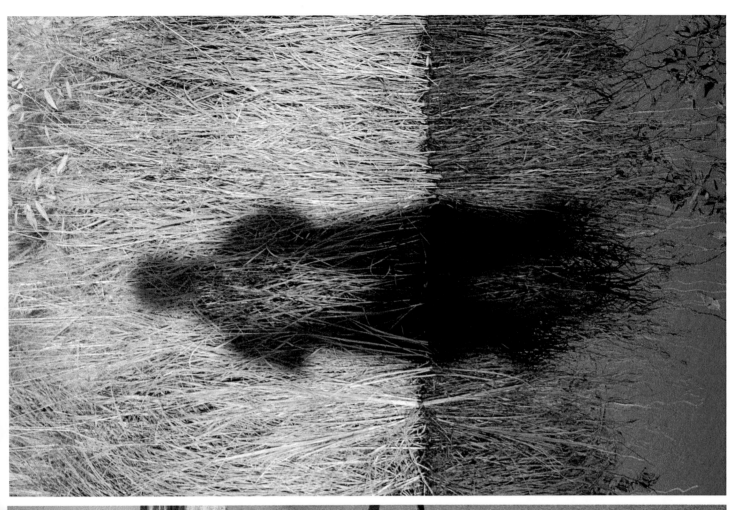

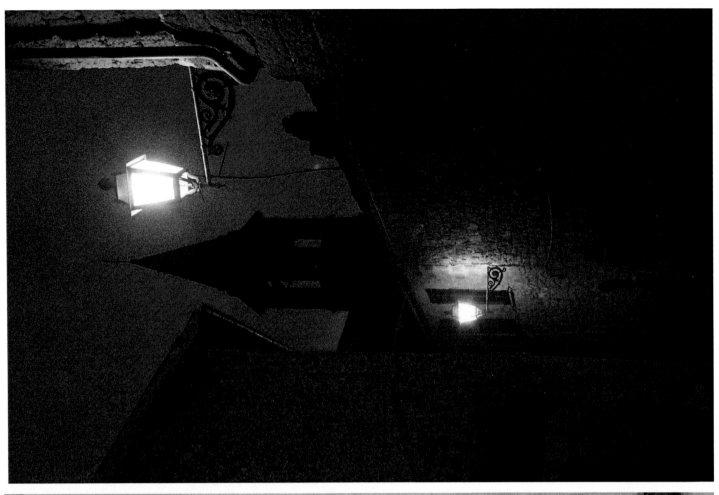

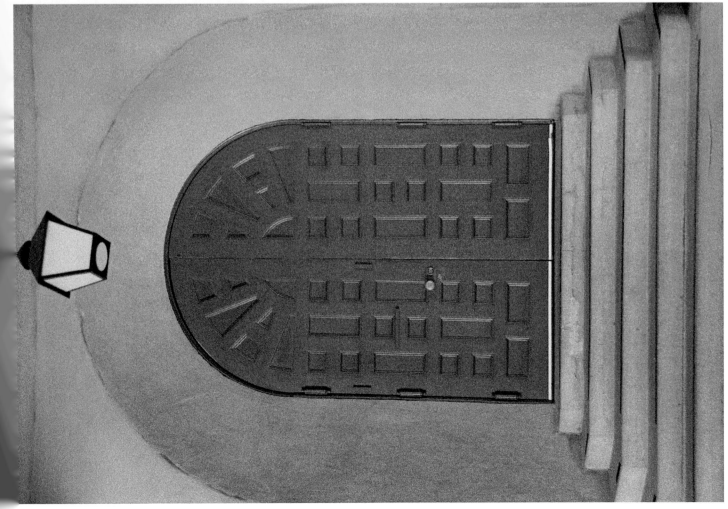

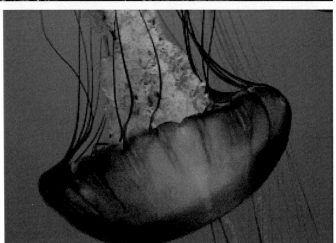

Do what
you want.
That's not selfish.
Selfish is
expecting
other people
to do
what you want.
Anthony DeMello

Once you have
chosen what
you cannot
complete
alone,
you are no
longer alone.

Course in Miracles

You are the whole ocean. Why send out for a sip of dew? Rumi

If you have
no anxiety,
the risk you
face is probably
not worthy of you.
Only risks you
have outgrown
don't frighten you.

David Viscott

My barn having
burned to the
ground,
I can now
see the moon.

Japanese saying

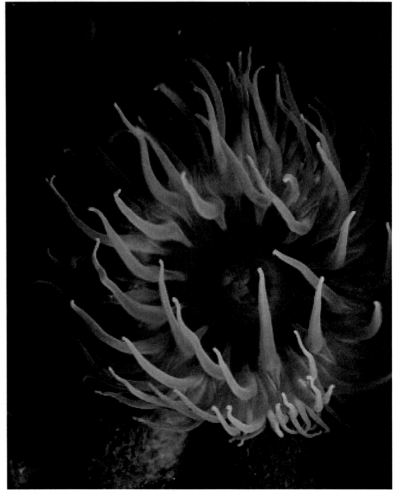

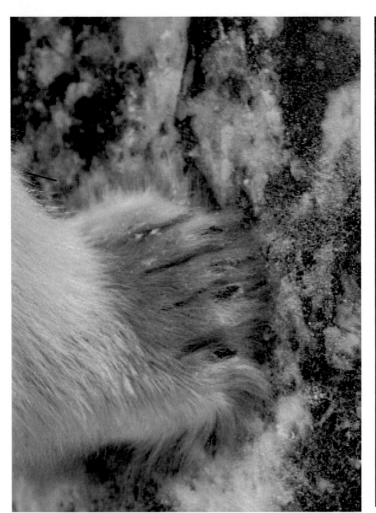

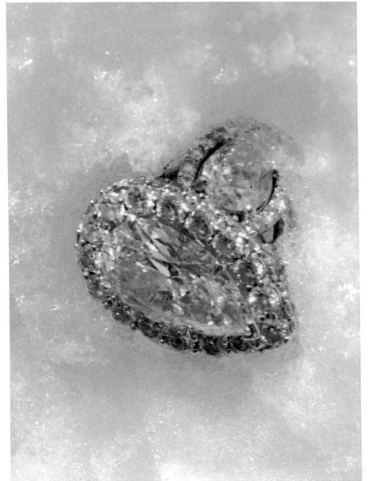

DARE GREATLY

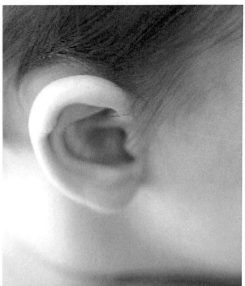

**There's someone out there who needs you.
Live your life so that person can find you.**
Balinese Dancer

Your own self-realization is the greatest
service you can render the world.
Ramana Maharshi

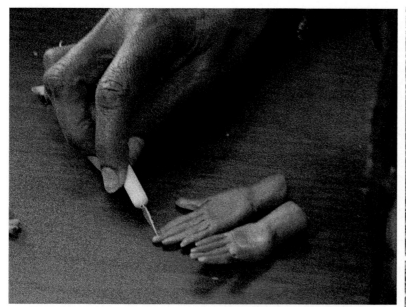
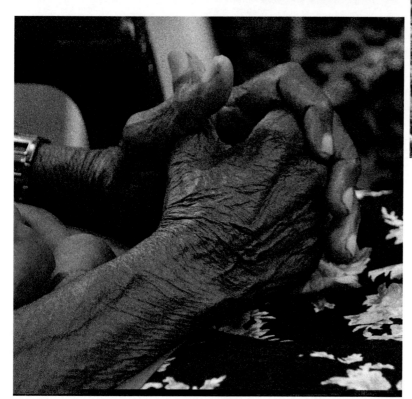

Jan Phillips is an award-winning author and photographer. She is also co-founder and CEO of the Livingkindness Foundation, sponsor of the annual Women's Voices, Women's Visions Symposium. She connects the dots between creativity, spirituality and inspired action. Jan is known for her multimedia presentations and for using the arts to keep the brain and heart connected. She creates a unique multi-sensory experience, weaving humor, storytelling, imagery, and music to ignite insights for life-changing action. Jan shows people how to access their wisdom and activate their creative energy. Her quest has led her into and out of a religious community, across the U.S. on a Honda motorcycle, and around the world on a one-woman peace pilgrimage. Blending east and west, art and activism, reflection and ritual, Jan's presentations provoke original thinking and prophetic action.

Jan is the author of *Finding the On-Ramp to Your Spiritual Path, Finding Ourselves on Sacred Ground, No Ordinary Time-The Rise of Spiritual Intelligence and Evolutionary Creativity, The Art of Original Thinking-The Making of a Thought Leader, Divining the Body, God Is at Eye Level-Photography as a Healing Art, Marry Your Muse, Making Peace: One Woman's Journey Around the World,* and editor of *A Waist is a Terrible Thing to Mind.* She has taught in over 25 countries and her work has appeared in the *New York Times, Ms., Newsday, People, Christian Science Monitor, New Age Journal, National Catholic Reporter* and *Utne Reader.*

Jan has three CDs of original music and several DVDs to inspire creativity.

For more info, www.janphillips.com; www.livingkindness.org

Made in the USA
San Bernardino, CA
08 December 2014